ESSENTIAL ELEMENTS

PIANO THEORY

T0079569

ISBN 978-1-4768-0610-5

HAL•LEONARD®
CORPORATION
7777 W. BLUEMOUND RD. P.O. BOX 13819 MILWAUKEE, WI 53213

In Australia Contact:
Hal Leonard Australia Pty. Ltd.
4 Lentara Court
Cheltenham, Victoria, 3192 Australia
Email: ausadmin@halleonard.com.au

Visit Hal Leonard Online at
www.halleonard.com

To the Student

I wrote these books with you in mind. As a young student I often wondered how completing theory workbooks would make me a better musician. The theory work often seemed separate from the music I was playing. My goal in *Essential Elements Piano Theory* is to provide you with the tools you will need to compose, improvise, play classical and popular music, or to better understand any other musical pursuit you might enjoy. In each "Musical Mastery" section of this book you will experience creative applications of the theory you have learned. The "Ear Training" pages will be completed with your teacher at the lesson. In this series you will begin to learn the building blocks of music, which make it possible for you to have fun at the piano. A practical understanding of theory enables you to see what is possible in music. I wish you all the best on your journey as you learn the language of music!

Sincerely,
Mona Rejino

To the Teacher

I believe that knowledge of theory is most beneficial when a concept is followed directly by a musical application. In *Essential Elements Piano Theory*, learning theory becomes far more than completing worksheets. Students have the opportunity to see why learning a particular concept can help them become a better pianist right away. They can also see how the knowledge of musical patterns and chord progressions will enable them to be creative in their own musical pursuits: composing, arranging, improvising, playing classical and popular music, accompanying, or any other.

A free download of the *Teacher's Answer Key* is available at www.halleonard.com/eeptheory3answer.

Acknowledgements

I would like to thank Hal Leonard Corporation for providing me the opportunity to put these theoretical thoughts down on paper and share them with others. I owe a debt of gratitude to Jennifer Linn, who has helped with this project every step of the way. These books would not have been possible without the support of my family: To my husband, Richard, for his wisdom and amazing ability to solve dilemmas; to my children, Maggie and Adam, for helping me think outside the box.

TABLE OF CONTENTS

REVIEW

1. Complete the music alphabet going forward and backward.

   A _ _ _ _ G F _ _ _ _ A

2. Trace the whole notes on the grand staff below. Write the letter name for each note in the blank. *The notes are skipping up by intervals of a 3rd.*

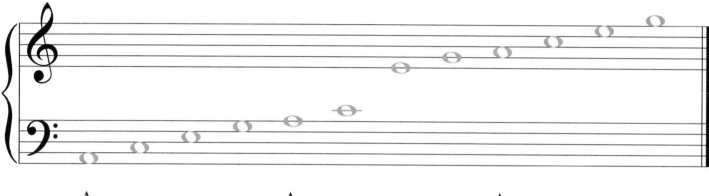

   A _ _ _ A _ _ _ A _ _ _

3. What recurring 4-note pattern did you discover? _____ _____ _____ _____

4. Name the following notes on the grand staff. Each measure will spell a word.

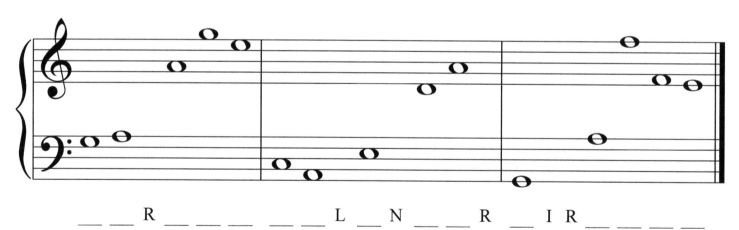

   _ _ R _ _ _ _ _ L _ N _ _ R _ I R _ _ _

5. Write the letter name of each note in the box below it.
   Name the interval in the blank (2nd, 3rd, 4th or 5th.)

A   C

_____3rd_____   _____   _____   _____

_____   _____   _____   _____

6. Draw whole notes to form melodic intervals from the given note. Name each note in the blank.

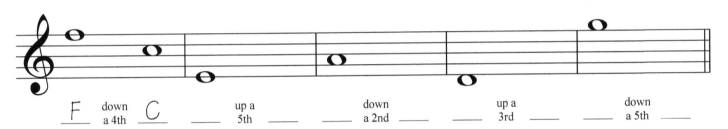

___F___ down   ___C___   _____ up a   _____   _____ down   _____   _____ up a   _____   _____ down   _____
      a 4th   5th   a 2nd   3rd   a 5th

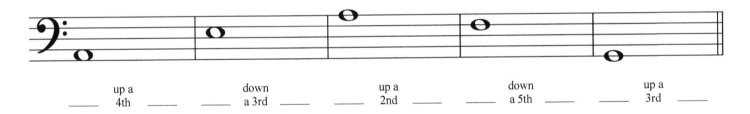

_____ up a   _____   _____ down   _____   _____ up a   _____   _____ down   _____   _____ up a   _____
      4th   a 3rd   2nd   a 5th   3rd

7. Write the name of each harmonic interval in the blank below it.

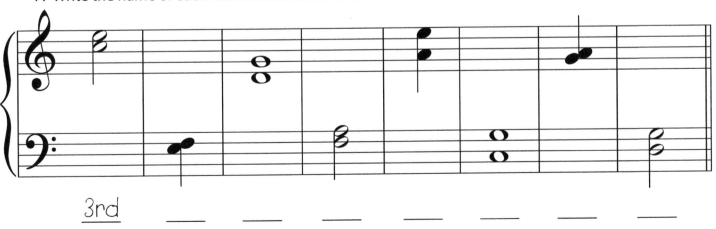

_____3rd_____   _____   _____   _____   _____   _____   _____

8. Follow the pattern given to complete the rhythm chart.

   Below each note or rest:

   a. Draw the note or rest.
   b. Name the note or rest.
   c. Write the number of counts the note or rest receives in $\frac{4}{4}$ time.

	♩	𝄽	𝅗𝅥	𝄼	𝅗𝅥.	𝅝	𝄻
a.	♩						
b.	quarter note						
c.	1 count						

9. Add all of the notes and rests as you would count them in $\frac{4}{4}$ time. Write the total number of beats in each box.

   1. ♩ + 𝅗𝅥 + 𝄼 + 𝄽 + 𝅝 = _____ beats

   2. 𝅗𝅥 + 𝄽 + 𝅗𝅥. + 𝄼 + ♩ = _____ beats

   3. 𝄻 + 𝅗𝅥. + 𝅝 + 𝄼 + ♩ = _____ beats

   4. 𝅗𝅥. + 𝅗𝅥 + 𝄽 + 𝄻 + 𝄼 = _____ beats

Rhythm and Time Signatures

♪ An **EIGHTH NOTE** = 1/2 beat of sound

♪ An **EIGHTH REST** = 1/2 beat of silence

Two or more eighth notes are joined together by a beam.

1. Add a flag to the quarter notes to make eighth notes. *Notice the flag always attaches to the right side of the stem.*

2. Add a beam to the quarter notes to make pairs of eighth notes.

3. Add a beam to the quarter notes to make groups of four eighth notes.

4. Trace the eighth rest, then draw four more.

♪

RHYTHM TREE

eight eighths = one whole

four eighths = one half

two eighths = one quarter

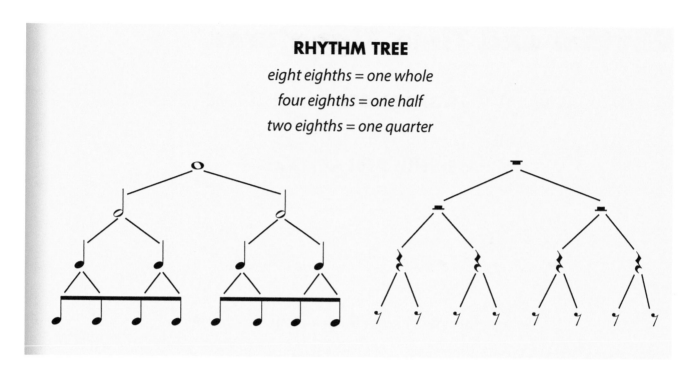

To count rhythms with **eighth notes**, divide each beat into two equal parts. Count the eighth note between the beats using the word "and."

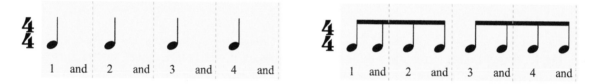

5. Clap and count the rhythms below, keeping a steady beat.

6. In each box draw **one note** that equals the total value of the eighth notes.

 =    =

 =    =

7. In each box draw **one rest** that equals the total value of the eighth rests.

 =    =

8. Write the counts below each measure. Use a + sign for the word "and." Clap and count each rhythm aloud.

$\frac{2}{4}$
1   +   2   +

$\frac{3}{4}$
1   +   2   +   3   +

$\frac{4}{4}$
1   +   2   +   3   +   4   +

9. Draw a line connecting the boxes that have the same number of beats.

10. Add bar lines to each rhythm below. Then write the counts below each measure.

11. Each measure below is incomplete. Draw **one note** in each box to complete the measure.

12. Each measure below is incomplete. Draw **one rest** in each box to complete the measure. *A whole rest equals one measure of silence in any time signature.*

Accidentals and Enharmonics

Sharps (♯), flats (♭) and naturals (♮) placed before notes are called **ACCIDENTALS**.

A **SHARP** sign means to play the closest key to the right, either black or white. Sharps go up.

1. Draw a sharp before each note. Then write the name of each note in the blank.

D♯ ___ ___ ___ ___ ___

A **FLAT** sign means to play the closest key to the left, either black or white. Flats go down.

2. Draw a flat before each note. Then write the name of each note in the blank.

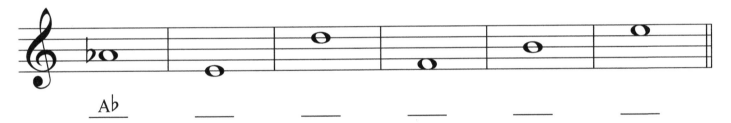

A♭ ___ ___ ___ ___ ___

A **NATURAL** sign cancels a sharp or flat. A natural is always a white key.

3. Draw a natural before the second note in each measure. Then write the name of each note in the blank.

C♯ C♮ ___ ___ ___ ___ ___ ___ ___

Accidentals affect every note on the same line or space for an entire measure. The bar line at the end of a measure cancels the accidental.

4. How many notes are played as C♯ in each measure? Write the correct number in the blank.

_____   _____   _____   _____

5. How many notes are played as B♭ in each measure? Write the correct number in the blank.

_____   _____   _____   _____

Notes may have two different names. Two notes that sound the same and have the same pitch, but are written differently are called **enharmonic** notes.

6. In the boxes below, write two names for each shaded key.

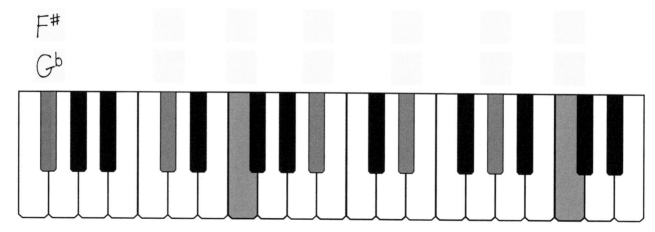

7. Name the enharmonic note for each given note.

B♭ = _____   F♯ = _____   E♭ = _____   C♯ = _____   F = _____

8. Draw the enharmonic note after each given note below.

9. Draw two enharmonic notes on each staff that name the shaded key.

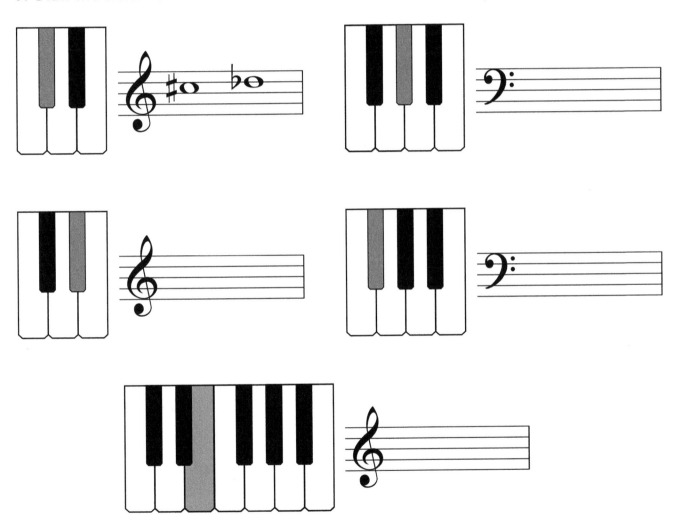

MUSICAL MASTERY

Ear Training

1. You will hear two groups of rhythm. There are two measures in each group. The first measure of each group is given. Fill in the second measure with the rhythm you hear.

2. You will hear one rhythm from each pair. Circle the rhythm you hear.

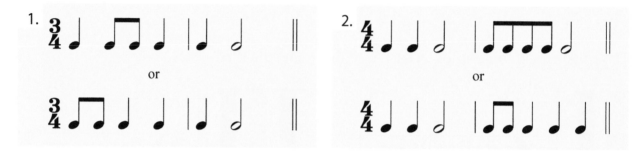

3. You will hear three groups of notes. The intervals will be either 2nds or 3rds. If you hear 2nds, circle the notes that step. If you hear 3rds, circle the notes that skip.

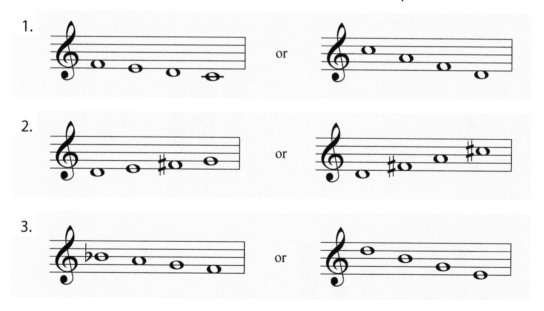

4. You will hear three notes in each group. The first two notes are written on the staff. After you hear the first two notes, write the missing third note in each measure. *The third note will repeat or go up or down by a 2nd (step) or 3rd (skip).*

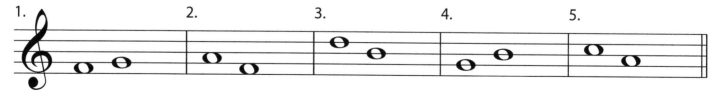

Rhythm Mastery

1. Draw **one note** in the empty box to balance each scale.

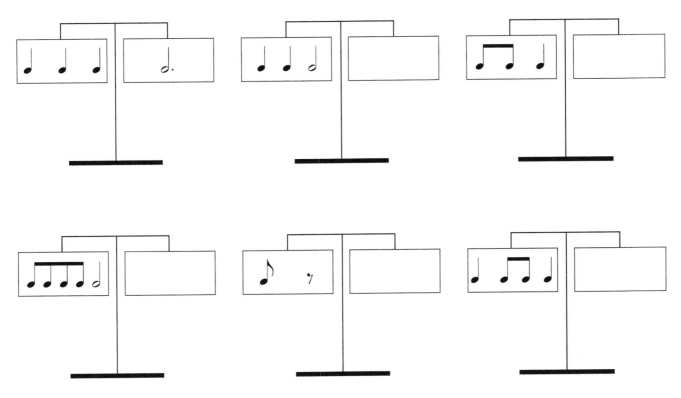

2. Draw **one rest** in the empty box to balance each scale.

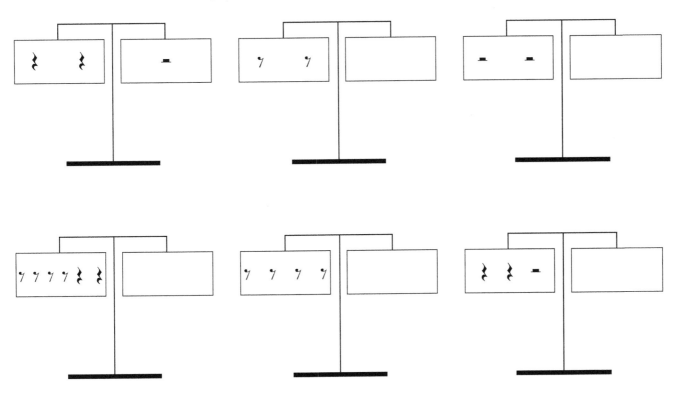

Reading Mastery

1. Show your mastery of eighth notes by playing "Rockin' Eighths."

Rockin' Eighths

Accompaniment (Student plays one octave higher than written.)

16

Half Steps and Whole Steps

A **HALF STEP** is the distance from one key to the very next key, with no key between.

HALF STEPS ON THE KEYBOARD

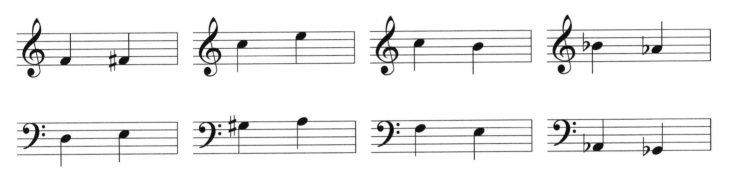

1. Circle the examples that contain half steps.

2. Draw whole notes a **half step higher** than the given notes. Use accidentals when needed. Name each note.

   C   C♯

3. Draw whole notes a **half step lower** than the given notes. Use accidentals when needed. Name each note.

   A   A♭

A **WHOLE STEP** is the distance from one key to another, with one key between. One whole step is two half steps combined.

WHOLE STEPS ON THE KEYBOARD

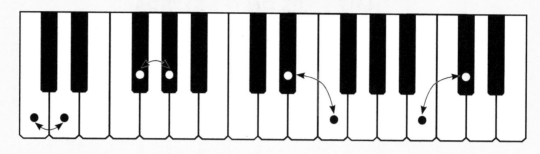

4. Circle the examples that contain whole steps.

5. Draw whole notes on the next line or space that are a **whole step higher** than the given notes. Use accidentals when needed. Name each note.

Bb   C   ___   ___   ___   ___   ___

6. Draw whole notes on the next line or space that are a **whole step lower** than the given notes. Use accidentals when needed. Name each note.

G#   F#   ___   ___   ___   ___   ___

7. Write **H** for half step and **W** for whole step in the boxes below the keyboard.

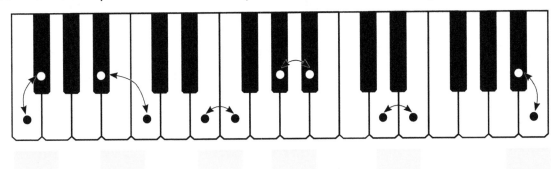

8. Write **H** for half step and **W** for whole step in the blanks below each pair of notes.

9. Circle the two notes that form a **half step** in each example.

10. Circle the two notes that form a **whole step** in each example.

Major 5-Finger Patterns and Triads

A **MAJOR 5-FINGER PATTERN** is made up of two whole steps, one half step, and another whole step. The half step is between the 3rd and 4th notes. The lowest note names the pattern.

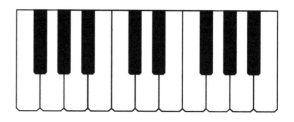

C Major 5-Finger Pattern

C D E F G
1 2 3 4 5

W W H W

G Major 5-Finger Pattern

G A B C D
1 2 3 4 5

W W H W

F Major 5-Finger Pattern

F G A Bb C
1 2 3 4 5

W W H W

1. Using a keyboard as a guide, complete the Major 5-finger patterns below. Use accidentals when needed. Mark the half steps with a curved line. *The first one is done for you.*

D Major

W W H W

A Major

W W H W

E Major

W W H W

A **TRIAD** is a three note chord. A **MAJOR TRIAD** is made up of the 1st, 3rd and 5th notes of a Major 5-finger pattern.

F Major 5-Finger Pattern

1   3   5

F Major Triad

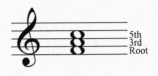

5th
3rd
Root

2. In the first measure, complete the Major 5-finger pattern. Mark the half step between the 3rd and 4th notes with a curved line. In the second measure, draw the Major triad for that pattern. *The first one is done for you.*

D Major 5-Finger Pattern   Triad

C Major 5-Finger Pattern   Triad

A Major 5-Finger Pattern   Triad

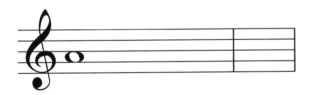

E Major 5-Finger Pattern   Triad

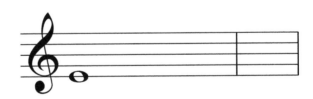

G Major 5-Finger Pattern   Triad

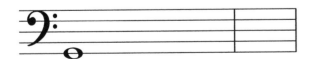

F Major 5-Finger Pattern   Triad

Minor 5-Finger Patterns and Triads

A **MINOR 5-FINGER PATTERN** is made up of one whole step, one half step, and two more whole steps. The half step is between the 2nd and 3rd notes. The lowest note names the pattern.

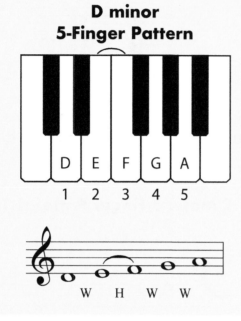

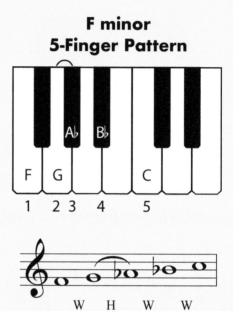

1. Using a keyboard as a guide, complete the minor 5-finger patterns on each grand staff below. Mark the half steps with a curved line.

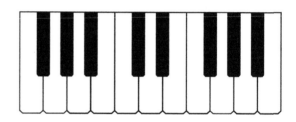

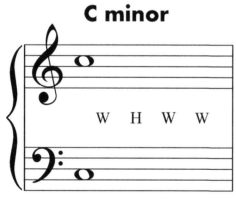

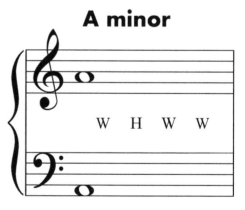

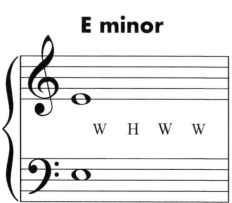

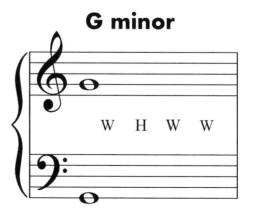

A **MINOR TRIAD** is made up the 1st, 3rd and 5th notes of a minor 5-finger pattern.

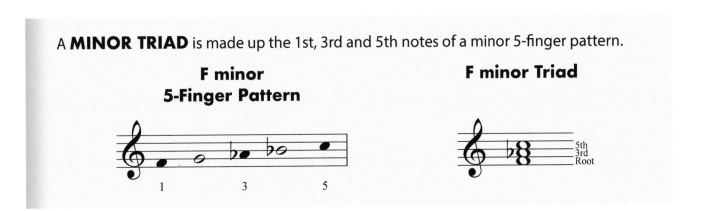

F minor 5-Finger Pattern

F minor Triad

2. In the first measure, complete the minor 5-finger patterns. Mark the half steps between the 2nd and 3rd notes with a curved line. In the second measure, draw the minor triad for that pattern.

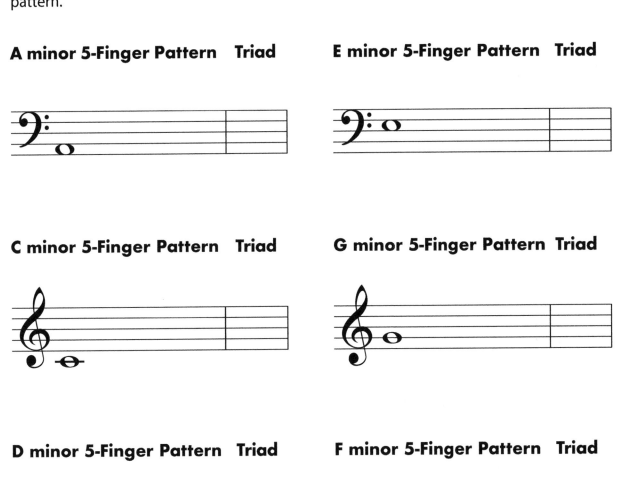

A minor 5-Finger Pattern   Triad

E minor 5-Finger Pattern   Triad

C minor 5-Finger Pattern   Triad

G minor 5-Finger Pattern   Triad

D minor 5-Finger Pattern   Triad

F minor 5-Finger Pattern   Triad

To change a **Major** 5-finger pattern into a **minor** 5-finger pattern, lower the third note one half step.

G Major 5-Finger Pattern Triad

G minor 5-Finger Pattern Triad

A Major 5-Finger Pattern Triad

A minor 5-Finger Pattern Triad

3. Play each pattern above. Listen to the difference in mood between the Major and minor patterns and triads.

4. Mark the half steps with a curved line in the patterns below. Then name each 5-finger pattern and triad in the box above it. Play each pattern.

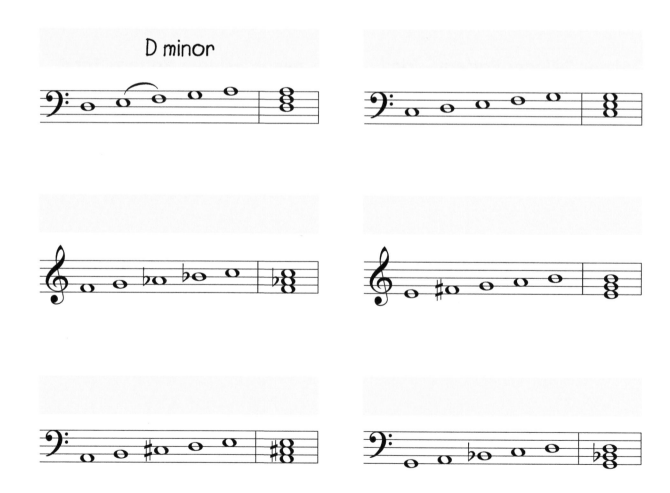

D minor

MUSICAL MASTERY

Ear Training

1. You will hear one melody from each pair. Circle the melody you hear.

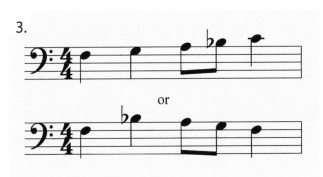

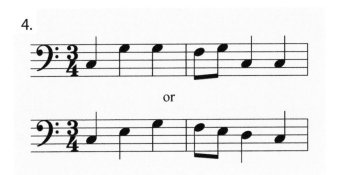

2. The first example in each pair is Major. The second example in each pair is minor. Circle the one you hear.

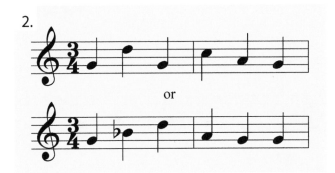

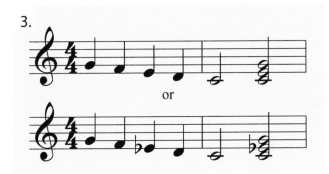

Reading Mastery

1. Place your hands in the C Major 5-Finger Pattern. Play "Ode to Joy."

Ode to Joy

Ludwig van Beethoven
(1770–1827)

2. Transpose "Ode to Joy." Place your hands in the G Major 5-Finger Pattern. Keep the intervals and rhythms the same. Play "Ode of Joy" in the G Major 5-Finger Pattern.

3. Transpose "Ode to Joy" to other 5-finger patterns. Choose from:

A MAJOR   **D MAJOR**   **F MAJOR**   **E MAJOR**

Reading Mastery: Identifying Major and Minor Patterns

Each melody below comes from a folk tune or classical work.

1. Play each melody. Then label each 5-finger pattern in the box above it. Choose from these patterns:

A Major	C Major	D Major	E Major
E minor	F Major	G Major	G minor

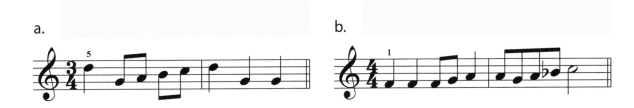

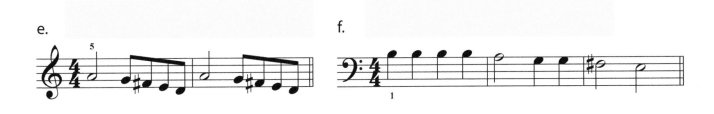

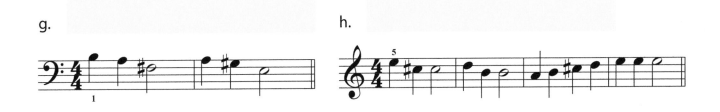

27

Musical Signs and Terms

An asterisk (*) indicates words that are new to this book.

DYNAMIC signs tell how soft or loud to play the music.

Italian Name	Sign (Symbol)	Meaning
pianissimo*	*pp*	very soft
piano	*p*	soft
mezzo piano	*mp*	medium soft
mezzo forte	*mf*	medium loud
forte	*f*	loud
fortissimo*	*ff*	very loud
crescendo* (cresc.)	◁	gradually louder
decrescendo or diminuendo* (dim.)	▷	gradually softer

1. In each blank write the dynamic sign to match the meaning.

   medium soft _____   very loud _____

   loud _____   soft _____

   very soft _____   gradually softer _____

   gradually louder _____   medium loud _____

TEMPO marks tell what speed to play the music.

Italian Name	Meaning
adagio	slow
andante	walking speed
moderato	moderate
allegro	fast (quickly and happily)
ritardando* (rit.)	gradually slower
a tempo*	return to the original tempo

2. In each blank write the Italian name for the following speeds.

walking speed _____   fast _____

gradually slower _____   moderate _____

slow _____   return to original tempo _____

ARTICULATION signs tell how to play and release the keys.

Name	Sign (Symbol)	Meaning
legato		play smoothly connected
staccato		play detached and separated
accent*		play louder; emphasize
tenuto*		hold full value; stress

Other Musical Symbols

D.C. al Fine

D.C. al Fine means to return to the beginning (*da capo*) and play to *fine* (the end).

A **tie** is a curved line that connects notes of the same pitch. Play only the first note and hold it for the combined value of both notes.

A **slur** is a curved line over or under two or more notes that are to be played legato (smoothly connected).

A **fermata*** means to hold a note longer than its rhythmic value.

8va

An **octave sign*** placed **above** the staff means to play one octave (eight notes) **higher** than written. An octave sign placed **below** the staff means to play one octave **lower** than written.

Repeat signs* mean to play the music between the repeat signs again.

1.   2.

1st and 2nd endings* mean to play the 1st ending and repeat from the beginning. Then skip over the 1st ending and play the 2nd ending.

The **pedal sign*** shows when to press and release the damper pedal (right pedal).

REVIEW

1. Match each symbol or term with its definition by writing the correct letter in the blank.

⌢ _____   a. very loud

ff _____   b. return to the beginning and play to *fine*

ritardando _____   c. gradually louder

accent _____   d. play eight notes higher or lower

staccato _____   e. hold longer than its rhythmic value

D.C. al Fine _____   f. very soft

◁ _____   g. gradually slower

a tempo _____   h. play louder; emphasize

tenuto _____   i. press and release the damper pedal

8va _____   j. play smoothly connected

⌞_____⌟ _____   k. return to the original tempo

pp _____   l. hold full value; stress

▷ _____   m. play detached and separated

accidentals _____   n. sharps, flats and naturals placed before notes

legato _____   o. gradually softer

2. Add all of the notes and rests as you would count them in $\frac{4}{4}$ time. Write the total number of beats in each box.

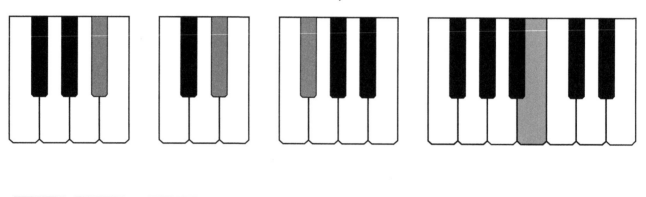

3. In the blanks write two names for each shaded key.

___ ___   ___ ___   ___ ___   ___ ___

4. Circle all the notes to be played as E-flat in the following example.

5. Write **H** for half step and **W** for whole step in the boxes below the keyboard.

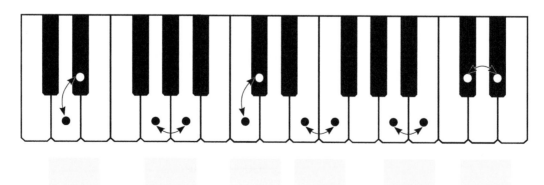

6. List the whole steps (W) and half steps (H) in the order they occur in a Major 5-finger pattern.

———————   ———————   ———————   ———————

7. List the whole steps (W) and half steps (H) in the order they occur in a minor 5-finger pattern.

———————   ———————   ———————   ———————

8. Name the following Major and minor 5-finger patterns. Draw the Major or minor triad for that pattern in the second measure.

———————   ———————————

———————   ———————————

———————   ———————————

———————   ———————————

MUSICAL MASTERY

Ear Training

1. You will hear three rhythm patterns that contain four measures each. Write the missing rhythm in the box.

2. You will hear three notes in each group. Write the missing third note on the staff.

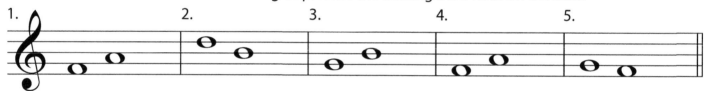

3. You will hear one melody from each pair. Listen carefully to the intervals, then circle the melody you hear.

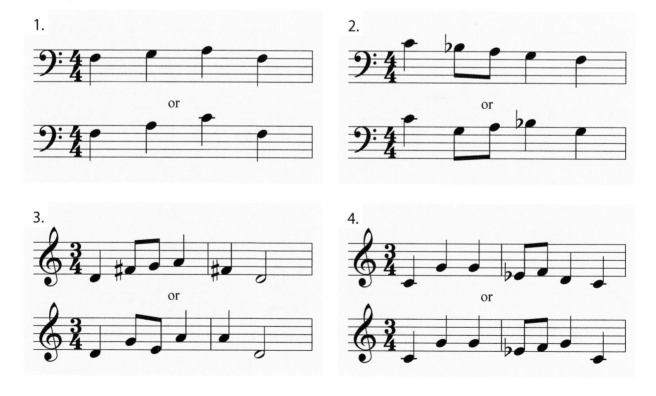

Analysis

Study this excerpt from "Gavotta," then answer the questions about it.

Gavotta
Op. 81, No. 3

James Hook
((1746–1827)

1. Name the dots over the quarter notes in measure 1. _____

2. Name the circled melodic interval in measure 8. _____

3. Do the half notes in measure 3 form a whole step or a half step? _____

4. How many eighth notes are in the bass clef? _____

5. What does the dynamic sign in measure 8 tell you to do? _____

6. Name the curved line over the notes in measures 7 and 8. _____

7. Name the circled 5-finger pattern in measure 2. _____

8. Name the circled 5-finger pattern in measure 4. _____

9. What is the meaning of "allegro?" _____

Symbol Mastery

Fill in the blanks with the correct answer. Choose from the terms and symbols in the box.

decrescendo	half step	♪	4th	accent
triad	♮	WWHW	tenuto	accidentals	slur
whole step	♫	crescendo	enharmonic	tie
legato	andante	WHWW	5th	ritardando	⌢

1. _____ means gradually slower.

2. Two notes that sound the same, but have different names are called _____.

3. An interval of a _____ skips three keys.

4. _____ equal one quarter note.

5. A _____ sign cancels a sharp or flat.

6. Sharps, flats and naturals are called _____.

7. The formula for a minor 5-finger pattern is _____.

8. _____ means hold the note full value, or stress the note.

9. The distance from one key to another with one key between is a _____.

10. A _____ is a curved line that means to play the notes *legato*.

11. _____ means gradually louder.

12. The distance from one key to the very next key is a _____.

THEORY MASTERY

Review Test

1. Complete the music alphabet going up and back down one time. Do not repeat the 7th letter.

   A ___ ___ ___ ___ ___ ___ ___ ___ ___ ___ ___ ___ ___

2. Draw the following notes. Use whole notes.

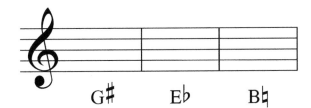 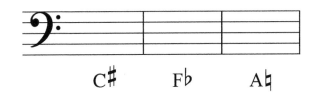

3. Name the enharmonic note for each given note.

   G# = _____   D# = _____   Bb = _____   Fb = _____   Db = _____

4. Write the name of each interval in the blank below it.

   ___ ___ ___ ___ ___ ___ ___ ___

5. On the staff below, draw the notes or rests that are named below each measure.

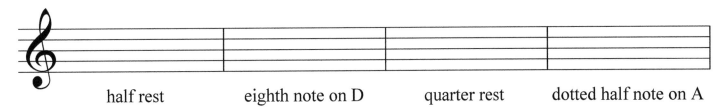

   half rest   eighth note on D   quarter rest   dotted half note on A

6. Write the name of each note in the blank below it.

   ___ ___ ___ ___ ___ ___

7. Write the counts below each measure.

8. Add **bar lines** and a **double bar line** where they are needed in the rhythm below.

9. Write the top number of the time signature in each measure below.

10. Write **H** for half step and **W** for whole step below each pair of notes.

11. Fill in the blanks with the correct number.

In a **Major** 5-finger pattern, the half step is between notes _____ and _____.

In a **minor** 5-finger pattern, the half step is between notes _____ and _____.

12. Name these Major and minor 5-finger patterns in the blanks below. Mark the half steps with a curved line.

13. Identify these Major and minor triads by writing their names in the blanks.

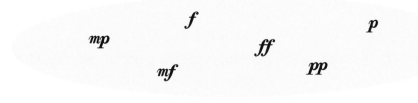

_____ _____ _____ _____ _____ _____ _____ _____ _____ _____

14. In the blanks below, arrange these dynamic signs in order from softest to loudest.

mp *f* *p* *ff* *mf* *pp*

_____ _____ _____ _____ _____ _____ _____

15. Match each term with its meaning or sign by writing the correct letter in the blank.

a. pedal sign _____

b. fermata _____

c. accent _____ play smoothly connected

d. octave sign _____

e. repeat signs _____ return to the original tempo

f. treble clef _____

g. ritardando _____ *8va*

h. slur _____ gradually softer

i. 1st and 2nd endings _____

j. bass clef _____ how soft or loud to play

k. dynamics _____ gradually slower

l. decrescendo _____

m. tenuto _____

n. a tempo _____

Ear Training

1. You will hear four measures of rhythmic dictation. Fill in the blank measures with the rhythm you hear.

2. You will hear four groups of notes. Circle the measure that matches exactly what you hear in each group.

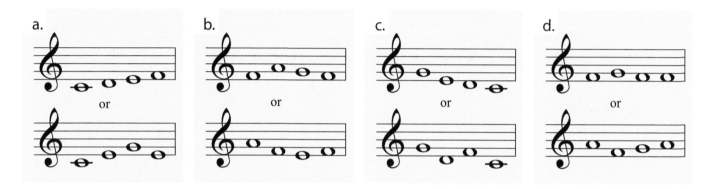

a.   b.   c.   d.

or   or   or   or

3. You will hear five sets of triads played in broken and blocked form. One of them is a Major triad. If the Major triad is the first chord played, circle 1. If the Major triad is the second chord played, circle 2.

1st set:	2nd set:	3rd set:	4th set:	5th set:
1 2	1 2	1 2	1 2	1 2

4. You will hear one interval from each pair. Circle the interval you hear.

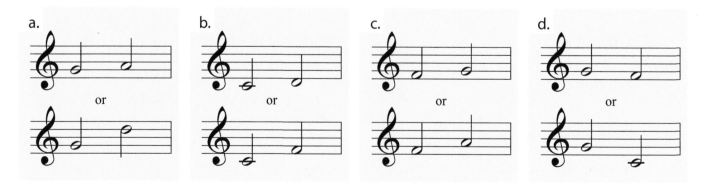

a.   b.   c.   d.

or   or   or   or